love food

love food

tina bester

PAVILION

contents

breakfasts

soups and salads

lunches

suppers

puddings

introduction

Love Food consists of a series of recipes for robust, heartwarming food and is crammed with ideas for meals that are the culinary equivalent of a lovely long hug.

The book is divided into five sections. There are recipes for moreish breakfast treats, the easiest soups and salads, hearty lunch offerings such as steak sandwiches with black pepper and mustard butter, flavour-packed suppers (many of them one-pot or one-dish wonders) and delightfully decadent puddings to make your own.

Many of the recipes have been passed down through the generations, with Tina Bester giving them her trademark twist. Offerings like old-school spaghetti and meatballs or retro-inspired lamb chops with cornflake crumbs are bound to become legends in your own household.

The recipes in *Love Food* are easy to follow, include no-nonsense advice and have been tried, tested and tweaked to perfection. You can rely on *Love Food* for mouthwatering, hearty offerings that are a contemporary take on the traditional.

breakfasts

creamy oats with fried banana and cinnamon sugar

I think of this as the ultimate comfort food.
Be generous with the cinnamon sugar.

100g/3½ oz/½ cup oats · 375ml/13fl oz/generous 1½ cups milk
250ml/8fl oz/1 cup water · pinch of salt
4 bananas · 1 tablespoon butter
4 tablespoons castor (superfine) sugar, mixed with
1 teaspoon ground cinnamon

Place the oats, milk, water and salt in a pot and bring to the boil.
Turn the heat down and slowly simmer the oats until they are thick and
creamy. Meanwhile, fry the bananas in the butter until golden brown.
Spoon the oats into bowls, place banana slices on top,
sprinkle with lots of cinnamon sugar and serve.

Serves 4

eggs benedict with wilted spinach

This recipe combines the best of two world-renowned egg breakfasts. The secret to the perfect poached egg is a good strong swirl in your saucepan of water.

50g /1 ³/₄oz/²/₃ cup baby spinach · toasted ciabatta · 2 slices bacon
I large egg · I teaspoon vinegar · pinch of salt
hollandaise sauce
225g/8oz/I cup butter · 3 large egg yolks
I tablespoon lemon juice · salt and pepper

Wilt the spinach in boiling water, drain and remove excess water.
Place it on top of the toasted ciabatta. Fry the bacon and meanwhile, break
the egg into a cup and bring a small pot of water to the boil. Add the vinegar
and a pinch of salt. Turn the heat off and swirl the water around with a spoon.
Carefully pour the egg into the middle of the swirl and allow it to settle.
Poach the egg for about 5 minutes. Place the egg on top of the bacon and make
the hollandaise sauce. Melt the butter until just bubbling. Place the egg yolks,
lemon juice and salt and pepper in a blender and with the blender running, slowly
add the hot butter. Stop the blender as soon as you have added all the butter.
Pour the hollandaise sauce over the poached egg and serve.

Serves I

soufflé omelette with smoked salmon, cream cheese and spring onion

The secret to the success of this all-day favourite is that
the egg white is well whisked before being reunited
with the yolk. Serve with crunchy whole-wheat toast.

6 large eggs, separated · salt and pepper
butter for frying · 100g/3½oz smoked salmon
100g/3½oz/scant ½ cup cream cheese
1 spring onion (scallion), thinly sliced

Preheat the oven to 180°C/350°F/Gas mark 4.
Beat the egg whites until light and fluffy and then add the egg yolks
and some salt and pepper. Melt the butter in two small ovenproof frying pans
and pour the mixture into the pans. Cook the omelettes on the hob (stove) until the
undersides are golden brown and then pop them into the oven for 3 minutes.
Remove the omelettes from the oven and top generously with
smoked salmon, dollops of cream cheese and spring onion.
Fold over and serve immediately with hot buttered toast.

Serves 2

flapjacks with honey and toasted almonds

A Sunday-morning special in our household –
it's the fluffiness that makes these flapjacks so moreish.

150g/5½ oz/1 cup self-raising flour • pinch of salt
¼ teaspoon bicarbonate of soda (baking soda) • 2 tablespoons sugar • 1 large egg
125ml/4½ fl oz/½ cup milk • 1 tablespoon vinegar • butter for frying
honey, toasted almonds and mascarpone (optional), to serve

Sift together the flour, salt, bicarbonate of soda and sugar.
Mix together the egg, milk and vinegar. Make a well in the middle
of the dry ingredients and slowly add the egg mixture, mixing with a
wooden spoon. Melt a knob of butter in a pan. Place spoonfuls of mixture
in the hot pan and flip each flapjack when the top starts to bubble.
Layer the flapjacks, drizzle with honey and top with toasted almonds.
Serve with a dollop of mascarpone for a little extra decadence.

Serves 2–3

ham, mozzarella and egg pan sandwiches

The essential accompaniment is a mug of strong tea.

butter · 8 slices white bread · 8 slices country ham
about 150g/5½ oz mozzarella, sliced
4 large eggs

Butter one side of all the slices of bread and place them
on a board, buttered-side down. Place two slices of ham on four
of the slices, as well as a generous portion of mozzarella. Fry the eggs
in butter in a hot pan and place the hot eggs on top of the cheese.
Place the remaining slices of bread on top of the eggs and
pan-fry the sandwiches on both sides until golden brown.

Serves 4

french toast with camembert and roasted vine tomatoes

The combination of sweet and savoury flavours
makes this a decadently delicious morning treat.

1 bunch vine tomatoes · olive oil
salt and pepper · 4 large eggs
100ml/3$\frac{1}{2}$fl oz/scant $\frac{1}{2}$ cup cream · 4 thick slices white bread
butter for frying · 1 Camembert round (about 125g/4$\frac{1}{2}$oz)
balsamic reduction (available from speciality food stores)

Preheat the oven to 180°C/350°F/Gas mark 4. Place the tomatoes in a roasting pan
and drizzle with a little olive oil. Season with salt and pepper and roast them
for 10 minutes. Mix the eggs and cream together in a bowl and season to taste.
Soak the bread in the egg mixture on both sides and fry in a buttered pan until
golden brown. Layer the French toast and top with half a Camembert round
and a sprig of roasted tomatoes. Drizzle with balsamic reduction and serve.

Serves 2

potato and bacon frittatas

Surprisingly simple to make, these are always
crowd pleasers at brunch.

3 potatoes, peeled and diced · 4 slices streaky (lean) bacon
6 large eggs · 250ml/8fl oz/1 cup fresh cream
30g/1oz/$^1/_4$ cup freshly grated Parmesan cheese
salt and freshly ground black pepper

Preheat the oven to 180°C/350°F/Gas mark 4. Lightly butter 12 muffin cups.
Cook the potatoes in salted water until tender, drain and
divide evenly among the muffin cups. Cut each slice of bacon into
3 pieces and place a piece on top of the potatoes in each muffin cup.
Mix together the eggs, cream, Parmesan and a good grinding of salt
and pepper. Carefully fill the muffin cups with the egg mixture.
Bake for 20–25 minutes until firm.

Makes 12

tomato relish and grilled cheese toasts

These take toasted cheese and tomato to new heights
and make a great breakfast or lazy Sunday supper.

1kg/2lb 4oz ripe tomatoes · 2 onions · 4 tablespoons vinegar
125ml/4fl oz/$\frac{1}{2}$ cup red wine · 4 tablespoons olive oil · 2 tablespoons sugar
salt and pepper · a few sprigs fresh thyme
about 200g/7oz/2 cups (tightly packed) Cheddar cheese, grated

Preheat the oven to 180°C/350°F/Gas mark 4. Wash, peel and chop
the tomatoes and onions and place them in a baking tray. Pour the vinegar,
red wine and oil over the tomatoes and onions. Sprinkle with sugar,
salt and pepper and mix gently. Tuck in the sprigs of thyme and bake,
stirring occasionally, for about 1½ hours or until the liquid has
almost cooked away and the tomatoes and onions have started to
go gooey. Adjust the seasoning if necessary. Smother 6 slices of toast
with the relish and top with grated cheese. Pop the toasts under the
grill (broiler) for 2–3 minutes until the cheese has melted and serve.

Serves 6

good old beans on toast

Everybody's favourite gets an extra kick thanks to the addition of
chilli and paprika. Bring the pan straight to the table
with thick slices of freshly toasted ciabatta.

2 onions, chopped · 1 tablespoon olive oil
2 x 400g/14oz tins whole peeled tomatoes
1 x 400g/14oz tin butter (lima) beans, drained and rinsed
1 x 400g/14oz tin borlotti (cranberry) beans, drained and rinsed
1 tablespoon balsamic vinegar
salt and freshly ground black pepper
3–4 teaspoons sugar · ½ teaspoon chilli flakes
1 teaspoon paprika

Fry the onions in the olive oil until just tender. Add the tomatoes,
break them up and cook gently for about 15 minutes. Stir in the
beans and vinegar and cook for another 5–10 minutes.
Season and stir in the sugar, chilli flakes and paprika.
Serve with toasted ciabatta.

Serves 4

soups and salads

french onion soup

This traditional soup fills any kitchen with a gorgeous aroma –
the thyme and dash of sherry make all the difference.

50g/1³/₄oz/scant ¹/₄ cup butter • 1kg/2lb 4oz onions, peeled and thinly sliced
1 tablespoon thyme • 3 tablespoons sherry
1.2 litres/2 pints/5 cups homemade chicken stock
salt and freshly ground black pepper

Heat the butter in a large pan and gently cook the onions and thyme
until the onions have softened but not browned (about 20 minutes).
Increase the heat slightly and cook for a further 15 minutes until the
onions become dark gold, sticky and caramelized, stirring regularly to
prevent them from catching. Add the sherry and simmer for 2–3 minutes,
then add the stock and bring to the boil. Season and simmer for 10 minutes.
Serve with grilled pecorino toasts made by heaping grated pecorino (romano) onto
slices of baguette and popping them under the grill (broiler) until golden brown.

Serves 6

leek and potato soup with crispy garlic pitas

The contrast between the smooth creamy soup and crunchy pita triangles never fails to please. This is one of Ali's favourites.

3 tablespoons butter · 6–8 leeks, well washed and sliced
125ml/4fl oz/½ cup white wine · 3 potatoes, peeled and sliced
3 cups chicken stock · salt and freshly ground black pepper
250ml/8fl oz/1 cup milk · 250ml/8fl oz/1 cup cream · sour cream, to serve
crispy garlic pitas
6 pita breads · 2 garlic cloves, crushed
4 tablespoons olive oil

To make the soup, melt the butter in a pot and fry the leeks until tender, adding a little white wine if the pot goes dry. Add the potatoes, about 2 cups of chicken stock and salt and pepper to taste. Cook until the potatoes are tender. Liquidize (blend) the soup and add the milk and cream. Adjust the seasoning if necessary, heat it through and serve with a drizzle of sour cream and the crispy garlic pitas.

To make the garlic pitas, preheat the oven to 180°C/350°F/Gas mark 4. Cut each pita bread into triangles and then split them. Mix the crushed garlic into the olive oil and generously brush the pitas with the garlic oil. Place them on a baking tray and toast them in the oven for 10 minutes.

Serves 6

roasted red pepper and tomato soup
with parmesan garlic bread

A recipe for a good tomato soup is an essential for every cook.
This one has extra zing courtesy of the roasted red peppers.

10 ripe tomatoes · 1 red (bell) pepper · olive oil
salt and freshly ground black pepper · 2 onions, peeled and chopped
3 garlic cloves, chopped · 1 tablespoon sugar · 500ml/17fl oz/2 cups water
4 tablespoons cream
parmesan garlic bread
1 loaf ciabatta 125g/4oz/$^1/_2$ cup butter, softened
50g/1$^3/_4$oz/$^1/_2$ cup Parmesan cheese, finely grated · 2 garlic cloves, crushed

Preheat the oven to 180°C/350°F/Gas mark 4. Cut the tomatoes in half and place
them cut-side up on a lined baking sheet. Cut the red pepper in half, remove the
seeds, cut each half into three pieces and add to the tomatoes. Drizzle with
olive oil and sprinkle with salt and pepper. Roast the tomatoes and red pepper for
45 minutes. Meanwhile, fry the onions in a little olive oil in a large pot. Remove the
tomatoes and red pepper from the oven, add to the onions and stir well. Add the
garlic, sugar and water and simmer for about 20 minutes. (This would be the perfect
time to assemble and bake the Parmesan garlic bread.) Place the soup in a blender
or food processor, blend it and then strain it through a sieve into a bowl to remove
all the pips and skins. Return it to the pot and add the cream. Heat through, adjust
seasoning and serve with warm Parmesan garlic bread.

To make the Parmesan garlic bread, cut 2cm/$^3/_4$inch slices into the ciabatta loaf
without slicing all the way through the bread. Combine the butter, Parmesan and
garlic and spread the mixture between the slices. Wrap the bread in baking paper,
fold in the ends and bake at 180°C/350°F/Gas mark 4 for 20 minutes.

Serves 6

butternut soup with chilli crème fraîche and roasted garlic toasts

A classic, butternut soup is good as a starter,
TV dinner or tasty winter lunch. You'll love this version's chilli twist.

2 onions, peeled and sliced · 2 tablespoons olive oil
1kg/2lb 4oz butternut squash, peeled and chopped · 1 litre/1¾ pints/4 cups water
2 garlic cloves, crushed · salt and freshly ground black pepper
125ml/4fl oz/½ cup cream
chilli crème fraîche
2 tablespoons crème fraîche · 1 teaspoon chilli paste
roasted garlic toasts
1 whole bulb garlic · olive oil · eight slices toast

Fry the onions in the olive oil until just tender. Add the butternut squash,
water and garlic. Season with salt and pepper and bring to the boil. Simmer until
the butternut is tender. Place the soup in the blender and blend until smooth.
Push it through a sieve (strainer) to remove any lumps. Stir the cream
into the soup, heat through and check seasoning.

To make the chilli crème fraîche, combine the crème
fraîche and the chilli paste and use to garnish the soup.

To make the garlic toasts, preheat the oven to 180°C/350°F/Gas mark 4. Slice the
garlic bulb in half across the middle, drizzle with a little olive oil and roast in the
oven for about 45 minutes until the garlic is soft and has a nutty smell and
flavour. Serve with slices of toast and bowls of hot butternut soup
garnished with chilli crème fraîche.

Serves 4

mom's minestrone

My mom often used to make this hearty Italian soup when we were kids –
the smell of it bubbling on the stove takes me straight back in time.

2 onions, peeled and sliced
1 green (bell) pepper, seeded and sliced
2 tablespoons olive oil · 2 garlic cloves, crushed
2 potatoes, peeled and cut into bite-sized chunks
2 carrots, peeled and sliced · 2 leeks, well washed and sliced
4 sticks celery, sliced · 2 tomatoes, chopped
1.5 litres/2¾pints/6¼ cups chicken (or vegetable) stock · 2 tablespoons tomato paste
2 teaspoons sugar · 100g/3½oz/1 cup shell pasta
1 x 400g/14oz tin butter (lima) beans, drained and rinsed
salt and freshly ground black pepper

Fry the onions and green pepper in the olive oil and then
add the garlic, potatoes, carrots, leeks, celery and tomatoes and fry
for a few minutes. Add the stock, tomato paste and sugar and cook
until the potatoes are just tender. Add the pasta and cook for
a further 20 minutes, then stir through the beans.
Season with salt and pepper and serve.

Serves 8

potato, bacon and spring onion soup

For me, this soup is just about the most
nurturing thing I could possibly eat. The secret
lies in the homemade chicken-stock base.

10 rashers (slices) streaky (lean) bacon, diced · olive oil
10 spring onions (scallions), chopped
10 potatoes, peeled and cut into bite-sized chunks
2 litres/3½ pints/8 cups homemade chicken stock
salt and freshly ground black pepper

Fry the bacon in a little olive oil and then add the spring
onions and cook for a few minutes. Add the potatoes and
stock and cook until the potatoes are soft but not mushy.
Add salt and pepper to taste at the end (not at the beginning, or
you may over-salt it because the bacon is quite salty).
Serve the soup hot with plenty of buttered toast.

Serves 6

hearty three-bean soup

This soup is perfect for long, lazy winter lunches sitting around a kitchen table. Serve it with chunks of well-buttered bread for delicious dipping.

2 onions, peeled and chopped
3 large carrots, peeled and sliced
olive oil · 2 x 400g/14oz tins whole peeled tomatoes
1 x 400g/14oz tin butter (lima) beans · 1 x 400g/14oz tin kidney beans
1 x 400g/14oz tin borlotti (cranberry) beans · 1 marrow bone (optional)
3 litres/5½ pints/12½ cups homemade chicken stock · 2 teaspoons sugar
salt and freshly ground black pepper

Fry the onions and carrots in a little olive oil until
just tender. Add the rest of the ingredients and bring to the boil.
Turn the heat down and simmer until the carrots are just tender.
Season with salt and pepper and serve. Note: the marrow bone can be
left out, and if you want a vegetarian soup, use vegetable stock
instead of the chicken stock.

Serves 6–8

asparagus, avocado and goat's cheese salad

Each of these three ingredients is special on their own –
put them together and you make real magic.
Serve this salad with a glass of cold, crisp white wine.

200g/7oz asparagus · olive oil · salt and freshly ground black pepper
2 ripe avocados · juice of 1 lemon · 100g/3¹/₂oz rocket (arugula)
200g/7oz chevin goat's cheese
honey and mustard vinaigrette
125ml/4fl oz/¹/₂ cup apple cider vinegar · 250ml/8fl oz/1 cup sunflower oil
1 garlic clove, crushed · 1 teaspoon honey
½ teaspoon mustard · salt and freshly ground black pepper to taste

In a hot griddle (grill) pan, sear the asparagus spears in a little olive oil and season
with salt and pepper. Peel the avocados, cut them in half and drizzle with a little
lemon juice to prevent them from discolouring. Place the halves on a bed of
crisp rocket, and top with the asparagus and goat's cheese.
Drizzle with the honey and mustard vinaigrette and serve.

To prepare the vinaigrette, place all the ingredients in
a bowl and whisk briskly to combine.

Serves 4

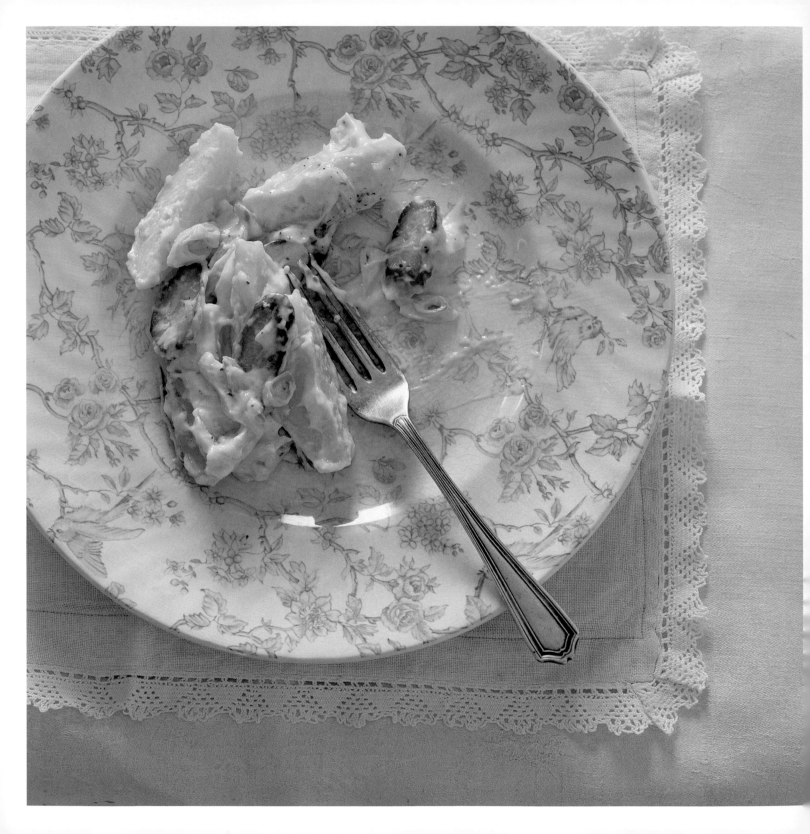

warm potato, pickle and spring onion salad

The secret of this salad is lashings of homemade mayonnaise.

10 potatoes, peeled · 4 spring onions (scallions), thinly sliced
4 pickled cucumbers (tea melons), thinly sliced
salt and freshly ground black pepper
4 tablespoons honey and mustard vinaigrette (see asparagus,
avocado and goat's cheese salad recipe)
homemade mayonnaise
2 eggs · salt and pepper to taste
1 teaspoon mustard (use whichever mustard you prefer)
2 tablespoons vinegar · 750ml/1$\frac{1}{4}$ pints/3 cups sunflower oil

Boil the potatoes in salted water until just done. Cut them into wedges
and place in a bowl with the spring onions (scallions), pickled cucumbers, seasoning,
mayonnaise and vinaigrette and gently toss to combine all the ingredients.
Adjust the seasoning and, if you like, add more mayonnaise.
Serve this salad warm or at room temperature.

To make the mayonnaise, blend the eggs, seasoning, mustard and vinegar together
in a food processor for 1 minute. With the food processor still running, slowly add
the oil in a thin stream (and think happy thoughts. I have been told that is the key
to mayonnaise success – just think happy thoughts, it works every time).

Serves 8

caramelized pear, gorgonzola and pecan nut salad

The robust flavours of these ingredients work together brilliantly, making this a great starter (appetizer). The grinding of black pepper on the pears is an essential flavour element.

2 tablespoons butter · 2 tablespoons sticky brown sugar
freshly ground black pepper · 2 pears · 100g/3½oz wild rocket (arugula)
200g/7oz Gorgonzola, cut into two wedges
100g/3½oz/⅔ cup pecan nuts, roughly chopped
1 quantity honey and mustard vinaigrette
(see asparagus, avocado and goat's cheese salad recipe)

Melt the butter and brown sugar in a pan and add a good grinding of
black pepper. Caramelize the pears in the pan until golden and sticky.
To assemble the salad, place a bed of tossed rocket on a plate and top
with the pears, wedges of cheese and chopped pecan nuts.
Drizzle with the honey and mustard vinaigrette and serve.

Serves 2

apple, crispy goat's cheese and grilled chicken salad

This combination of warm, crunchy goat's cheese, crisp apple slices and grilled chicken is simply wonderful.

4 skinless chicken breast fillets · 4 tablespoons olive oil, plus extra for frying
2 garlic cloves, crushed · salt and freshly ground black pepper
100g/3½oz/⅔ cup watercress
4 crisp green apples, cored and thinly sliced · juice of 1 lemon
crispy goat's cheese
200g/7oz chevin goat's cheese · 2 tablespoons flour · 2 large eggs, lightly beaten
60g/2oz/scant ½ cup dried breadcrumbs · 2 tablespoons olive oil
yoghurt dressing
4 tablespoons Bulgarian yoghurt · 3 tablespoons honey and mustard
vinaigrette (see asparagus, avocado and goat's cheese salad recipe)

Combine the chicken breasts with 4 tablespoons olive oil,
crushed garlic, salt and pepper and leave it to stand for at least 1 hour.
Sear the chicken breasts in a hot griddle (grill) pan until just done.

To make the crispy goat's cheese, cut each 100g/3½oz chevin roll into 6 pieces.
Dust with the flour, dip each piece in the beaten egg and then coat them in
breadcrumbs. Pan-fry the rounds in a little olive oil until golden brown
(1–2 minutes on each side).

To make the dressing, combine the yoghurt and vinaigrette.

To assemble the salad, top a bed of watercress with the seared
chicken breasts, slices of apple tossed in a little lemon juice and crispy
goat's cheese rounds. Drizzle with the yoghurt dressing and serve.

Serves 4

lunches

salmon fishcake burgers with wasabi and lime mayonnaise

One of the most extravagant fish burgers around, but well worth the effort. Someone once told me that the secret of good mayonnaise is to think happy thoughts while making it – and it has worked every time.

500g/1lb 2oz salmon · 2 tablespoons olive oil
salt and freshly ground black pepper
300g/10½oz potatoes, boiled and roughly mashed
zest of 2 lemons · 4 tablespoons fresh coriander (cilantro), chopped
1 large egg · 150g/5½oz/generous 1 cup dried breadcrumbs
2 large eggs, beaten · vegetable oil for frying
8 fresh bread rolls

wasabi and lime mayonnaise
2 large eggs · 2 tablespoons lime juice · zest of 3 limes
½ teaspoon wasabi paste (available from Asian food stores)
salt and freshly ground black pepper to taste
about 750ml/1¼pints/3 cups vegetable oil

Preheat the oven to 200°C/400°F/Gas mark 6. Place the salmon on a baking sheet lined with baking paper, drizzle with olive oil, season and bake for 15 minutes. Allow it to cool and flake it into pieces. Add the roughly mashed potatoes, lemon zest, coriander, 1 egg and 1 cup of breadcrumbs and combine them well.

(CONTINUES ON NEXT PAGE)

(CONTINUED FROM PREVIOUS PAGE)

Shape them into patties, dip them in the beaten egg and then
in the remaining breadcrumbs and fry them until golden brown
(about 2–3 minutes on each side). Serve the burgers on fresh
bread rolls with lashings of wasabi and lime mayonnaise.

To make the mayonnaise, place all the ingredients except
the oil in a food processor and process them for about 1 minute
until well combined. With the processor running, slowly
add the oil until the mayonnaise has emulsified.

Makes 8

parmesan-crusted chicken burgers

The crust is made using a decadent mix of grated Parmesan,
fresh parsley and fresh breadcrumbs. Delicious served with rocket, chives
and hot mustard mayonnaise.

200g/7oz/scant 1½ cups dried breadcrumbs
50g/1¾oz/generous ¾ cup parsley, finely chopped
50g/ 1¾oz/½ cup grated Parmesan cheese • salt and pepper
4 skinless chicken breast fillets • flour for dusting
2 large eggs, lightly beaten • olive oil for frying • 4 fresh bread rolls
fresh rocket (arugula) leaves, to serve • fresh chives, to serve
hot mustard mayonnaise
125ml/4fl oz/½ cup homemade mayonnaise (see warm potato,
pickle and spring onion salad recipe)
1 tablespoon hot English mustard

Combine the breadcrumbs, parsley and Parmesan in a bowl.
Salt and pepper the chicken breasts and dip them in the flour,
then in the beaten egg and finally coat with the breadcrumb mixture.
Fry them in olive oil until just done (about 3–4 minutes on each side).

To make the mustard mayonnaise, combine the mayonnaise with the mustard.

To assemble the burgers, warm the rolls in the oven for a few minutes,
spread liberally with the mayonnaise, top with rocket and chives and
add a crisp chicken breast to each one.

Makes 4

steak, rocket and onion ring sandwiches on sourdough bread

The pesto mayonnaise adds a mouthwatering zing
to this otherwise classic combination of flavours.

400g/14oz porterhouse steak · salt and freshly ground black pepper
olive oil · sourdough bread · rocket (arugula), to serve
onion rings
2 onions, peeled and thickly sliced · 500ml/17fl oz/2 cups milk
150g/5½oz/1 cup flour · 50g/1¾oz/generous ⅓ cup cornflour (cornstarch)
1 teaspoon baking powder
1 teaspoon castor (superfine) sugar · 1 teaspoon salt
330ml/11floz/generous 1¼ cups beer · vegetable oil for frying
pesto mayonnaise
4 tablespoons mayonnaise · 1 teaspoon pesto

Pat the steak dry with paper towel (a Julia Child tip).
Season the meat and fry in a little olive oil until done to your liking.

To make the onion rings, separate the rings, place them in the milk
and leave them to soak for 20 minutes. Combine the rest of the
ingredients except the oil in a bowl and whisk together to make the
batter. Remove the rings from the milk, dip them in the batter
and fry in the hot oil until golden brown.

(CONTINUES ON NEXT PAGE)

(CONTINUED FROM PREVIOUS PAGE)

To make the pesto mayonnaise, mix the
mayonnaise and pesto together until well combined.

To assemble the sandwiches, slice the bread and generously spread
with the pesto mayonnaise. Top with rocket, place the steak on top of
the rocket and finish off with the onion rings.

Serves 2

balsamic honey chicken, bacon and camembert sandwiches

These are a real treat thanks to the combination of sweet and salty flavours, oozy Camembert and crunchy peppery watercress.

salt and freshly ground black pepper · 4 skinless chicken breast fillets
olive oil · 12 slices streaky (lean) bacon · 4 tablespoons balsamic vinegar
3 tablespoons honey · 1 baguette · watercress, to serve
2 Camembert rounds (about 125g/4½oz each)

Season the chicken fillets and cut them into strips.
Heat a little olive oil in a large frying pan and add the chicken and
bacon. Fry for a minute and then add the balsamic vinegar and honey
and cook until it is sticky and caramelized. To assemble the sandwiches, slice
the baguette lengthways down the middle, butter it and top it with watercress.
Layer on the bacon and chicken and top with slices of Camembert.
Cut into 4 portions to serve.

Serves 4

beef fillet sandwiches with black pepper and mustard butter, shoestring chips and caramelized onions

Beer bread is so easy to make and is exactly what's needed as a base for this flavour fest.

beer bread
360g/12¼oz/generous 2⅓cups plain (all-purpose) flour · 3 teaspoons baking powder
2 teaspoons salt · 375ml/13fl oz/generous 1½ cups beer

black pepper and mustard butter
50g/1¾oz/scant ¼ cup butter, softened · 2 tablespoons mustard
1 garlic clove, crushed · 2 teaspoons finely chopped fresh parsley
½ teaspoon paprika · 2 teaspoons freshly ground black pepper

shoestring chips
800g/1lb 12oz potatoes, peeled · vegetable oil for frying · salt

1kg/2lb 4oz fillet (tenderloin) steak · freshly ground black pepper
4 tablespoons olive oil · 6 onions, peeled and thinly sliced
2 tablespoons olive oil · rocket (arugula), to serve
6 pickled cucumbers (tea melons), sliced, to serve

To make the beer bread, preheat the oven to 190°C/375°F/Gas mark 5. Combine the flour, baking powder and salt in a bowl. Make a well in the centre and gradually add the beer to form a dough, stirring it with a butter knife.

(CONTINUES ON NEXT PAGE)

(CONTINUED FROM PREVIOUS PAGE)

Place the dough on a lightly floured surface and knead for five minutes.
Place the bread in a loaf tin (pan) and bake for about 1 hour.

To make the black pepper and mustard butter, combine all
the ingredients in a bowl and refrigerate until needed.

To make the chips, use a zester to cut the potatoes into long strings.
Pat them dry and heat the oil in a saucepan. Fry the potato strings in
batches until golden brown (about 2 minutes). Drain them on
absorbent paper and sprinkle with sea salt.

Season the fillet steak with black pepper and fry in 4 tablespoons olive oil
until done to your liking. Allow the meat to rest and in the meantime,
fry the onions in 2 tablespoons olive oil until sticky and caramelized.

To assemble the sandwiches, slice the beer bread, spread with mustard
butter and top with rocket, generous slices of fillet, pickles and a spoonfull
of caramelized onions. Serve with the shoestring chips.

Serves 6

club sandwiches with grilled chicken, bacon, soft boiled egg and 'cheat's' caesar dressing

Use streaky bacon (it gets lovely and crisp) and drizzle generously with the oh-so-simple Caesar dressing for lunchtime decadence.

salt and freshly ground black pepper
4 skinless chicken breast fillets
olive oil · 8 slices streaky (lean) bacon · 4 large eggs · butter, to serve
2 ciabatta rolls, broken in half · rocket (arugula), to serve
50g/1¾oz pecorino (romano), shaved, to serve
'cheat's' caesar dressing
4 tablespoons mayonnaise · 3 tablespoons vinaigrette
1 anchovy, chopped (optional)

Season the chicken breasts and fry them in a little oil in a hot griddle pan until just done. Fry the bacon and at the same time boil the eggs in a pot of boiling water for 8 minutes. To assemble the sandwiches, butter each half of the rolls and top with rocket, a chicken breast, two slices of bacon, pecorino shavings, a halved soft boiled egg and a good drizzle of dressing.

To make the 'cheat's' Caesar dressing, place all the ingredients in a blender and blend for a few seconds.

Serves 4

smoorsnoek with crusty bread

This South African staple gets a contemporary update with the addition of fresh ginger. Sweet, fruity chutney is a must with this one.

3 potatoes, peeled · vegetable oil · 1 onion, peeled and sliced
2 tablespoons finely chopped fresh ginger
1.5kg/3lb 5oz smoked snoek (or smoked mackerel), de-boned, skinned and flaked
freshly ground black pepper

Boil the potatoes until just done, allow them to cool and cut into bite size pieces. Fry the cubed potatoes in vegetable oil until they start to turn brown and then set them aside. Fry the onion and ginger in a little oil, then turn the heat right down. Place the flaked fish on top of the onions, layer the potatoes on top and season with a good grind of black pepper. Keep warm for about 20 minutes. Mix together gently and serve with chunky bread and chutney.

Serves 6

bangers with balsamic onions and mustard mash

Flavourful balsamic reduction gives these
grilled bangers a deliciously sweet kick.

4 pork bangers (sausages) · 1 onion, peeled and cut into wedges
balsamic reduction (available from speciality food stores)
olive oil · 3 potatoes, peeled · 4 tablespoons fresh cream
1 teaspoon mustard · 1 tablespoon butter
salt and freshly ground black pepper

Preheat the oven to 180°C/350°F/Gas mark 4. Place the bangers and onion wedges
in a roasting pan and drizzle generously with balsamic reduction and
olive oil. Roast them in the oven for about 25 minutes. To make the mash,
boil the potatoes, mash them well and push them through a sieve (strainer)
for extra-smooth mash. Add the cream, mustard, butter, salt and a good grind of
black pepper and combine well. Drizzle with a little olive oil before
serving with the bangers and balsamic onions.

Serves 2

marrow on toast

You either love or hate this dish – and I love it
for being quick, easy and so very delicious.

12 marrow bones
salt and freshly ground black pepper
olive oil

Preheat the oven to 180°C/350°F/Gas mark 4. Place the marrow bones on a baking
sheet and season with salt and pepper. Drizzle generously with olive oil and
roast in the oven for about 1 hour. Serve hot with lots of toast.

Serves 4

chicken with lemon and olives

This is so easy to make and the classic Mediterranean flavours
make it a really scrumptious treat.

2 red onions, peeled and cut into wedges
8 garlic cloves, unpeeled · 1 lemon, cut into thin wedges
250ml/8fl oz/1 cup white wine · 4 chicken thighs · 4 chicken drumsticks
olive oil · salt and freshly ground black pepper
100g/3½oz/generous ½ cup kalamata olives, pitted

Preheat the oven to 180°C/350°F/Gas mark 4. Place the onion, garlic, lemon,
wine and chicken pieces in a roasting pan. Drizzle with olive oil and
season with salt and pepper. Bake for 45 minutes, remove from the
oven, add the olives and return to the oven for a further 10 minutes.
Take the chicken out of the roasting pan and keep warm.
Reduce the pan juices on the hob (stove) to make a deliciously lemony sauce.
Serve with fluffy basmati rice or couscous.

Serves 4

suppers

pot-roast lamb with crisp roasted baby potatoes

I think that pot-roasting is one of the best ways to cook lamb.
It cooks in all its own juices and stays deliciously succulent.

2 tablespoons olive oil · 1 large leg of lamb
Worcester sauce · 10 whole baby carrots, peeled
10 baby onions, peeled · 250ml/8fl oz/1 cup white wine
salt and freshly ground black pepper
crisp garlic potatoes
1.5kg/3lb 5oz baby potatoes · 125ml/4fl oz/¹/₂ cup olive oil
12 garlic cloves · Maldon salt

Preheat the oven to 180°C/350°F/Gas mark 4. Place the olive oil in an oven proof
pot and brown the leg of lamb with a little Worcester sauce. Don't add salt while you
are browning the meat because it will draw liquid and then it ends up boiling. Place
the carrots and onions in the pan and add the white wine. Season the meat and
vegetables, place the pot in the oven with the lid on and cook for 30 minutes.
Turn the heat down to 110°C/225°F/Gas mark ¹/₄ and cook for a further 8 hours.

To roast the potatoes, preheat the oven to 180°C/350°F/Gas mark 4. Boil the
potatoes in a big pot of boiling water until they are just cooked through. Drain them
and squash them with the back of a spoon. Toss them with the olive oil and Maldon
salt and place them in a roasting pan. Roast for 25–30 minutes until crisp.

Serves 6–8

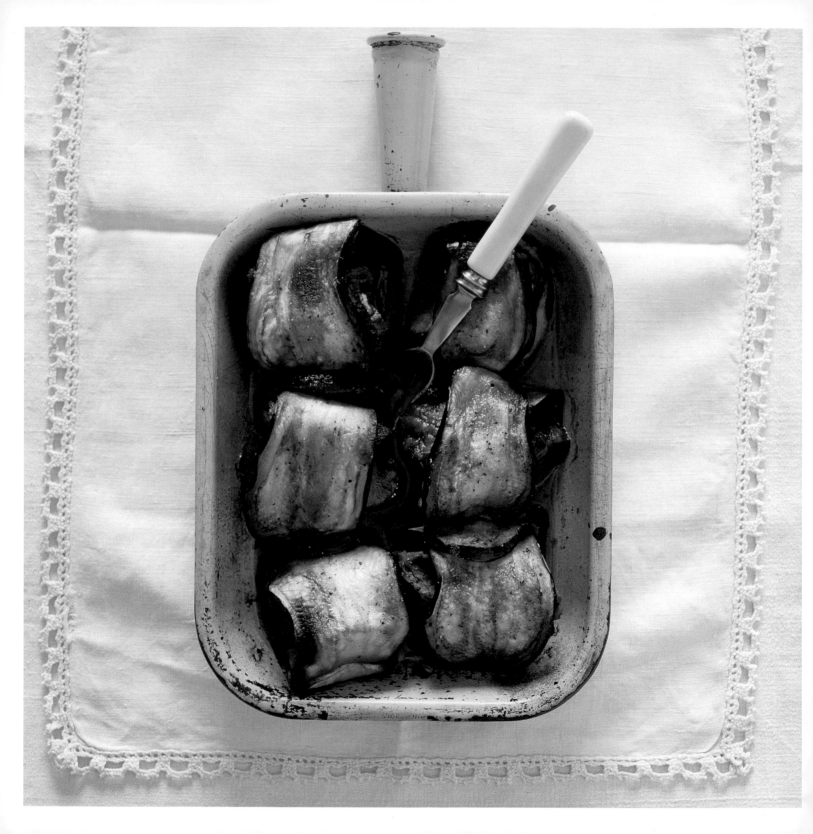

slow-roasted leg of lamb wrapped in aubergine

A delicious combination of rich roast lamb and creamy aubergine –
just pop it into the oven and forget about it.

1 leg of lamb, de-boned
salt and freshly ground black pepper
2–3 aubergines (eggplants), thinly sliced lengthways

Preheat the oven to 180°C/350°F/Gas mark 4. Cut the de-boned lamb into
8 portions and season each piece. Wrap each piece of lamb in slices of aubergine,
using toothpicks to hold them in place, and sprinkle with more salt and pepper.
Place the lamb portions in a roasting pan, cover with foil and bake for
30 minutes, then turn the heat down to 110°C/225°F/Gas mark ¼ and continue
cooking very slowly for about 8 hours. Don't add any extra liquid to the pan because
the lamb will make its own juices.
Remove the toothpicks before serving.

Serves 6–8

potato bake

This is seriously creamy, dreamy stuff and one of
those dishes where seconds (and thirds) are inevitable.
Serve it with a gorgeous green salad to balance its richness.

10 potatoes, peeled · salt and freshly ground black pepper
1 litre/1¾ pints/4 cups fresh cream · 3 bay leaves

Preheat the oven to 180°C/350°F/Gas mark 4.
Thinly slice the potatoes and layer them in a dish.
Sprinkle each layer with salt and pepper.
Pour the cream over the potatoes, top with the
bay leaves and bake for about 1 hour until the
potatoes are cooked through.

Serves 6–8

shepherd's pie

Using individual serving dishes for this ultracomforting
classic makes for a smart kitchen supper.

3 onions, peeled and thinly sliced · 3 tablespoons olive oil
1kg/2lb 4oz beef mince (ground beef) · 3 x 400g/14oz tins whole peeled tomatoes
3 garlic cloves, crushed · 2 tablespoons sugar
salt and freshly ground black pepper · 250ml/8fl oz/1 cup water
6 potatoes, peeled and chopped
4 tablespoons cream · 2 tablespoons butter

Fry the onions in the olive oil until soft and then add the mince and fry it until
it is nicely browned. Add the tomatoes, garlic and sugar and season with salt
and pepper. Add the water and gently simmer for about 1 hour until the mince is
completely cooked. Preheat the oven to 180°C/350°F/Gas mark 4. Boil the potatoes
until soft and then mash them with a potato masher; I always also push them through
a sieve to get really smooth mash. Add the cream and half the butter and season with
salt and pepper. Place spoonfuls of the mince mixture into individual bowls (or one
big one) and top with dollops of mashed potato. Dot knobs of the rest of the butter
on top and bake in the oven for 20–25 minutes until golden brown on top.

Serves 8

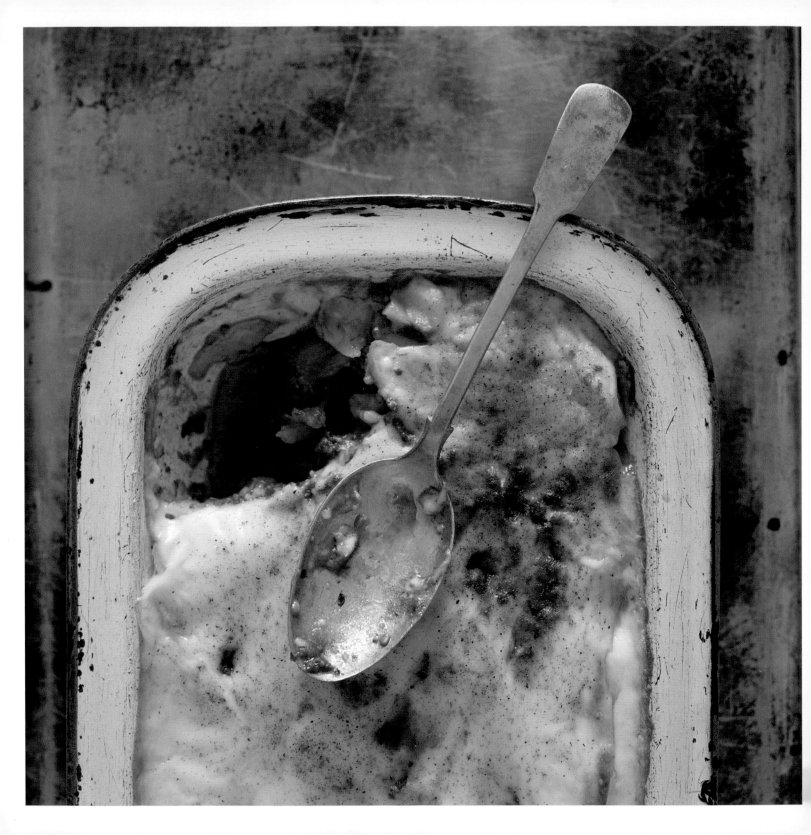

moussaka

One of those dishes of which one helping is never enough –
and eaten by the spoonful straight out of the fridge the
next day, it's even better!

salt and freshly ground black pepper
4 aubergines (eggplants), sliced · olive oil
8 potatoes, peeled
1 portion basic mince mixture (see shepherd's pie recipe)
ground nutmeg
béchamel sauce
125g/4½oz/generous ½ cup butter · 125g/4½oz/generous ¾ cup flour
1 litre/1¾ pints/4 cups milk

Preheat the oven to 180°C/350°F/Gas mark 4. Season the aubergine and fry in the
olive oil until just crispy. Boil the potatoes until tender, allow to cool and then slice
lengthways. To assemble the moussaka, layer the mince, aubergine and potatoes and
then repeat the layers, ending with a layer of mince. Pour the béchamel sauce over
the moussaka and dust with a little nutmeg. Bake for 30 minutes until it starts to
bubble around the edges. Serve with fluffy basmati rice.

To make the béchamel sauce, melt the butter in a pot, add the flour and
combine well. Slowly add the milk, stirring it with a whisk to remove any lumps.
Cook the sauce until it has thickened, stirring it all the time.

Serves 8

chicken paprika

This is such an easy dish, yet it's full of rich, spicy flavours.

1 whole chicken · 3 tablespoons olive oil
juice of 1 lemon · salt and freshly ground black pepper
250ml/8fl oz/1 cup water · 2 onions, peeled and sliced
2 tablespoons oil · 1 tablespoon butter
10 rashers (slices) bacon, chopped · 250ml/8fl oz/1 cup white wine
4 tablespoons paprika · 2 tablespoons tomato paste
1½ tablespoons sugar · 500ml/17fl oz/2 cups cream

Preheat the oven to 180°C/350°F/Gas mark 4. Place the chicken in a roasting pan and drizzle with 3 tablespoons olive oil and the lemon juice. Season with salt and pepper. Add the water to the pan and roast for 1½ hours. Allow the chicken to cool and remove all the meat from the bones. (This can all be done in advance.) Fry the onions in 2 tablespoons olive oil and the butter until tender, adding a little water if the pan goes dry. Add the bacon and fry until crisp. Turn up the heat and when it is really hot, add the wine and cook for 5 minutes. Add the paprika, tomato paste and sugar. Stir and cook for a few minutes to allow the flavours to develop. Add the cream and the chicken and allow it to simmer gently for about 5 minutes. Serve hot with spaghetti.

Serves 8

lamb curry

Waxy potatoes and pearl onions are the perfect partners
in this flavoursome lamb curry.

vegetable oil · 2kg/4lb 8oz lamb knuckles
Worcester sauce · about 375ml/13fl oz/generous 1½ cups red wine
freshly ground black pepper · 20 baby onions
8 potatoes, peeled and sliced into wedges · salt
500ml/17fl oz/2 cups chicken stock · 250ml/8fl oz/1 cup red wine
curry paste
4 tablespoons medium-strength curry powder
½ teaspoon chilli · 2 teaspoons ground coriander
2 tablespoons mustard seeds · 2 tablespoons chopped fresh ginger
2 tablespoons sugar · 125ml/4fl oz/½ cup chutney · 8 allspice berries
3 sticks whole cinnamon · 6 garlic cloves, crushed

Place a little oil in a large pot, get it really hot and brown the lamb knuckles.
Add a little Worcester sauce and a little red wine at a time when the pot
goes dry. Make sure that the lamb does not boil in the red wine. Add some
ground black pepper while you are browning the meat. Remove the knuckles
from the pot and brown the onions, also adding a little red wine if necessary.
Remove from the pot. Mix all the curry paste ingredients together and place
in the pot. Gently simmer for a minute so that all the flavours can blend.
Place the meat back in the pot, put the onions on top and then
add the potatoes. Season with salt, add the chicken stock and 250ml/8fl oz/1 cup
red wine and simmer on a very low heat for about 2 hours.

Serves 8

spaghetti and meatballs with roasted tomato, red onion and basil sauce

As any gran will tell you, it's the little bit of sugar that's the
essential ingredient in this baked tomato sauce.
Another of Ali's all-time favourites.

500g/1lb 2oz/4½ cups beef mince (ground beef)
150g/5½oz/3 cups fresh breadcrumbs
1 onion, peeled and grated · 2 tablespoons Worcester sauce
2 tablespoons chutney · 1 egg
salt and freshly ground black pepper to taste
600–800g/1lb 5oz–1lb 12oz spaghetti
roasted tomato, red onion and basil sauce
2 red onions, peeled and chopped
2 tablespoons olive oil · 2 x 400g/14oz tins whole peeled tomatoes
2 garlic cloves, crushed · 30g/1oz/scant ½ cup basil · 2 teaspoons sugar
salt and freshly ground black pepper to taste

To make the tomato sauce, fry the onions in the olive oil until just tender and then
add the rest of the ingredients. Bring to the boil and simmer gently for about
45 minutes. To make the meatballs, preheat the oven to 180°C/350°F/Gas
mark 4. Mix the mince, breadcrumbs, grated onion, Worcester sauce, chutney,
egg and seasoning together in a bowl. Lightly shape the mixture into 8 large balls
and place them in an oven dish. Cover with the tomato sauce and bake for about
45 minutes. In the meantime, cook the pasta in a large pot of boiling salted water.
Serve the freshly cooked pasta with plenty of sauce and meatballs.

Serves 6–8

gran's chicken tetrazzini

This dish takes me straight back to my gran's breakfast nook.
I call it 'heaven in a pan' and because it uses chicken stock rather
than cream, you can eat twice as much with half the guilt.

1 roast chicken · 1 tablespoon olive oil · 10 slices streaky (lean) bacon, chopped
1 green (bell) pepper, seeded and finely sliced
8–10 spring onions (scallions), chopped
4 black mushrooms, peeled and sliced
2 tablespoons flour · 625ml/21fl oz/2½ cups homemade chicken stock
salt and freshly ground black pepper · 500g/1lb 2oz spaghetti

Remove all the meat from the chicken and set it aside. Heat the oil in a pan and
fry the bacon until crisp. Remove from the pan and fry the green pepper for a few
minutes, then add the spring onions. Fry for a few more minutes, then add the
mushrooms. Add the chicken and heat through. Remove from the heat, sprinkle
the flour over the chicken mixture, and slowly add the stock, stirring gently to make
sure that no lumps of flour form. Once all the flour is mixed in, return the pan to
the heat and cook gently until the stock has thickened slightly. Season to taste and set
aside. In the meantime, cook the spaghetti until just done, pour off the water and
add the sauce to the spaghetti. Stir together gently and serve.

Serves 4–6

mom's lamb chops with cornflake crumbs

This is my favourite dish in the whole world.
Once you've tried these chops you'll also be hooked.

salt and freshly ground black pepper
8 lamb loin chops (allow 2 or more chops per serving)
cornflake crumbs

Season the chops and coat with crumbs on both sides.
Place under a hot grill (broiler) in the oven for about 30 minutes,
turning the chops halfway through the cooking time.
Sprinkle a few extra crumbs on the chops when you turn them.
Serve with boiled potatoes, sweet carrots and creamed spinach.

Serves 4

slow-cooked pork and beans

Everyone loves a savoury, slow-cooked stew, especially with chunks of crusty bread to mop up all the lovely sauce.

500g/1lb 2oz dried butter (lima) beans, soaked overnight
2 onions, peeled and chopped · 4 carrots, peeled and sliced
2 stalks celery, chopped · 2 tablespoons olive oil
3 garlic cloves, crushed
4 sprigs each of sage, thyme and rosemary,
tied together with a piece of string
800g/1lb 12oz pork, cut into 2cm/¾inch cubes · freshly ground black pepper
250ml/8fl oz/1 cup white wine · 3 ripe tomatoes, peeled and chopped · salt

Drain and rinse the beans and then drain again. Fry the onions, carrots and celery gently in the olive oil for about 10 minutes. Add the garlic, herbs and pork and enough water to come halfway up the ingredients. Add a good grinding of black pepper (but no salt). Turn the heat down and simmer gently for 1½ hours. Add the drained beans, the white wine and a little more water to cover the beans and simmer for a further hour. Add salt to taste and the tomatoes, and simmer for another 30 minutes until both beans and pork are tender.
Serve with warm chunks of crusty bread.

Serves 4–6

coq au vin

A one-pot-wonder that's twice as nice eaten cold the next day.
I like to serve it with large helpings of buttery mash.

4 chicken thighs · 4 chicken drumsticks
olive oil · 12 pearl onions
750ml/1¼ pints/3 cups red wine · 3 bay leaves
salt and freshly ground black pepper

Brown the chicken pieces in a little olive oil in a large pot.
Remove the chicken from the pot, add a little more oil and brown the onions.
Place the chicken back in the pot along with the red wine and bay leaves and
season with salt and pepper. Cover and cook for about 1 hour until
the chicken is soft and tender.

Serves 4

puddings

bread and butter pudding

The buttered croissants make this dish extra indulgent –
leave it to stand for at least an hour before baking to ensure that
the custard soaks into every nook and cranny.

4 croissants, sliced · butter
apricot jam (jelly) · 2 tablespoons raisins · 3 large eggs
100g/3¹/₂oz/¹/₂ cup sugar · pinch of nutmeg
1 teaspoon vanilla extract
500ml/17fl oz/2 cups warm milk

Cut the croissants into diagonal slices and spread butter and jam on each slice.
Layer them in a lightly greased baking dish and sprinkle each layer with raisins
(but don't put raisins on the top, as they will burn). Beat the eggs, sugar, nutmeg
and vanilla together in a bowl and then pour the warm milk onto the egg mixture,
beating all the time. Make sure that all the sugar has dissolved. Pour the mixture
through a strainer and then pour it over the croissants and allow it to stand for
at least 1 hour before cooking. (This is important otherwise it ends up
tasting very 'eggy'.) Preheat the oven to 180°C/350°F/Gas mark 4 while
the pudding is standing and bake for about 30–45 minutes.

Serves 6–8

ultimate steamed chocolate pudding
with chocolate fudge sauce

Seriously decadent and gorgeously gooey – you'll never need
another chocolate pud recipe. And don't be afraid of steamed
puddings, they are surprisingly easy to get right.

180g/6$\frac{1}{8}$oz/generous $\frac{3}{4}$ cup butter, melted, plus extra for greasing
6 large eggs · 240g/8$\frac{1}{2}$oz/scant 1$\frac{1}{4}$ cups castor (superfine) sugar
140g/5oz/scant 1 cup flour
85g/3oz/generous $\frac{3}{4}$ cup cocoa powder (unsweetened cocoa)
250g/9oz/9 squares dark chocolate, finely chopped
chocolate fudge sauce
250ml/8fl oz/1 cup double (heavy) cream
145g/5$\frac{1}{8}$oz/generous $\frac{5}{8}$cup butter · 40g/1$\frac{1}{2}$oz/scant $\frac{1}{4}$ cup sticky brown sugar
175g/6oz/6 squares dark chocolate

Grease a pudding bowl well with butter (make sure the bowl will fit into
your largest pot). In a separate bowl, beat the eggs and sugar together.
Sift the flour and cocoa powder together and add the egg and sugar mixture
to the dry ingredients. Mix it carefully, making sure that you don't
knock out all the air. Fold in the melted butter and chopped chocolate and
pour into the greased bowl. The next part sounds complicated but it's not.
Take two layers of greaseproof (waxed) paper and make a pleat in the middle.

(CONTINUES ON NEXT PAGE)

(CONTINUED FROM PREVIOUS PAGE)

Place over the top of the bowl and tie it firmly around the top with string.
Cover with foil and tuck the edges of the foil under the greaseproof (waxed) paper.
Place in a large pot and pour in enough boiling water to come halfway up
the bowl. Bring to the boil and then place the lid on the pot. Steam the pudding
for 1 hour and 45 minutes, checking it regularly to ensure that the pot doesn't
boil dry. Once the pudding is ready, serve it straight out of the bowl with
plenty of chocolate fudge sauce and thick cream or vanilla ice cream.

To make the chocolate fudge sauce, place the cream, butter and sugar in
a double boiler and heat gently, stirring, until the butter has melted.
Add the chocolate and stir all the time until it has melted and all
the ingredients are well combined.

Serves 6–8

mom's crème caramel

This is the best pudding for breakfast!
One spoonful is never enough, especially when you're dipping into
it the next day – a practice that in our family we call 'evening off'
(as in, 'I'm just evening off the edges').

caramel
200g/7oz/1 cup sugar · 125ml/4fl oz/$^1/_2$ cup water
custard
750ml/1$^1/_4$ pints/3 cups milk · 6 large eggs
125g/4$^1/_2$oz/scant $^2/_3$ cup sugar · 1 teaspoon vanilla extract

Preheat the oven to 180°C/350°F/Gas mark 4. To make the caramel, melt the sugar
and water and allow it to caramelize, but watch it very carefully so that it doesn't burn
and don't stir it or it will crystallize. Pour it into a mould and using oven gloves to
hold the mould, swirl the caramel around to line the inside of the mould. You have
to work very quickly, as the caramel sets within a few minutes. To make the custard,
warm the milk but do not let it boil. Beat the eggs and pour the warm milk over the
eggs, beating them all the time. Add the sugar and vanilla extract and beat them well
to make sure that all the sugar has dissolved. Pour the egg mixture into the mould
through a strainer, as the egg whites can sometimes be a bit stringy. Place the mould
in an oven dish with enough water to come halfway up the sides of the mould
and bake for about 30–40 minutes. A tester or knife will come out clean
when it is done. To un-mould the crème caramel, loosen all the
edges and then slip a knife down the side to release the vacuum.
Place a plate over the top, flip and pop it out of the mould.

Serves 6–8

banana fritters with caramel sauce

Hot battered banana treats drizzled with caramel –
what more do you need in life?

125g/4¹/₂oz/cup/scant I cup flour · pinch of salt · ¼ teaspoon turmeric
250ml/8fl oz/I cup chilled sparkling mineral water
vegetable oil for frying
4 bananas, peeled and cut lengthways
vanilla mascarpone, to serve
caramel sauce
100g/3¹/₂oz/¹/₂ cup (solidly packed) brown treacle sugar
250ml/8fl oz/I cup fresh cream
I teaspoon vanilla extract · I tablespoon butter

Place the flour, salt and turmeric in a bowl and whisk in the mineral water
until the batter is just combined. Heat the oil in a pan, dip the banana halves
in the batter and fry for I minute on each side. Drain them on paper towel and
serve immediately with the caramel sauce and dollops of vanilla mascarpone.

To make the caramel sauce, place all the ingredients in a saucepan and bring
to a slow simmer. Cook for 5 minutes until the sauce is thick and syrupy.

Serves 4

turkish delight semifreddo

I love the smooth texture and the subtle
sweetness the rose-water brings.

3 large eggs · 2 large egg yolks
200g/7oz/1 cup castor (superfine) sugar · 400ml/14fl oz/1¾ cups fresh cream
1 teaspoon rose-water
200g/7oz Turkish delight, chopped

Place the eggs, egg yolks and sugar in the top of a double boiler and heat,
whisking continuously, for about 5 minutes until the mixture is thick and pale.
Remove from the heat and beat with electric beaters for 10 minutes until it
has cooled. Set it aside and in the meantime, beat the cream until it forms
soft peaks. Fold the cooled egg mixture through the cream. Pour it into a cake
pan and swirl through the rose-water and the Turkish delight.
Cover the tin with clingfilm (plastic wrap) and freeze overnight.

Serves 6–8

raspberry and almond trifle

I add a generous splash of almond liqueur to this –
it gives the trifle a gloriously fragrant taste.

1 x 20cm/8-inch vanilla sponge cake (a store-bought cake is fine)
125ml/4floz/$^1/_2$ cup amaretto · 250ml/8fl oz/1 cup raspberry jam (jelly)
500g/1lb 2oz/3$^1/_3$ cups fresh raspberries
500ml/17fl oz/2 cups cream, lightly whipped
100g/3$^1/_2$oz/1 cup flaked (slivered) almonds, toasted

vanilla custard

500ml/17fl oz/2 cups milk · 1 teaspoon vanilla extract, or the seeds of 1 vanilla pod
5 large egg yolks · 50g/1$^3/_4$oz/$^1/_4$ cup castor (superfine) sugar · 2 tablespoons flour

Line the bottom of a large trifle bowl or individual bowls with the sponge cake
and drizzle with the amaretto. Spread generously with raspberry jam and sprinkle
over half the fresh raspberries. Pour the hot custard over the raspberries and
allow it to cool. Top with the whipped cream, toasted almonds and the rest
of the fresh raspberries.

To make the custard, warm the milk and vanilla in a pot but make sure the
mixture doesn't boil. In a separate bowl, beat the egg yolks and sugar and add the
flour, beating it well to make sure that there are no lumps. Pour the warm milk
mixture into the egg mixture, beating all the time. Pour into the top of a double
boiler through a strainer and cook until the custard has thickened.

Serves 6–8

127

banoffee pie

This is the pudding that no one ever wants to admit they like to eat but let's face it – everybody loves it. I use ginger biscuits for extra retro fabulousness.

150g/5$^{1}/_{2}$oz ginger biscuits (cookies), crushed · 85g/3oz/$^{3}/_{8}$ cup butter, melted
8 bananas, peeled and sliced
500ml/17fl oz/2 cups fresh cream, whipped
caramel
1 x 400g/14oz tin condensed milk
3 tablespoons golden (corn) syrup · 60g/2$^{1}/_{4}$oz/generous $^{1}/_{4}$ cup butter

Mix the crushed ginger biscuits and butter together and use to line the base of a pie dish (or individual dishes). Place in the fridge to set. To assemble the pie, spread the caramel over the base, then top with the bananas and the whipped cream.

To make the caramel, place the condensed milk, golden syrup and butter in a pot and heat until the ingredients are well combined, stirring all the time to make sure it doesn't catch. Turn the heat down and cook until the mixture thickens, stirring all the time.

Serves 6–8

'eat and mess'

This meringue and berry wonder has its origins in the
halls of the famous Eton school but since Ali was little it's only
ever had this name in our house.

6–8 plain or chocolate-swirl meringues (store-bought meringues are fine)
500ml/17fl oz/2 cups fresh cream, whipped
250g/9oz/1²/₃ cups fresh strawberries, hulled

Roughly crush the meringues into a big bowl and add the whipped cream.
Stir together gently and top generously with the strawberries.

Serves 6–8

conversion table

MEASUREMENTS

Standard	Metric
¼ inch	5mm
½ inch	1cm
1 inch	2.5cm
2 inches	5cm
3 inches	7cm
4 inches	10cm
5 inches	12cm
6 inches	15cm
7 inches	18cm
8 inches	20cm
9 inches	23cm
10 inches	25cm
11 inches	28cm
12 inches	30cm

LIQUID MEASURE

Standard	Metric
1 teaspoon	5ml
1 tablespoon	15ml
1 dessertspoon	2 teaspoons
¼ cup	60ml
⅓ cup	80ml
½ cup	125ml
⅔ cup	160ml
¾ cup	175ml
¾ cup	180ml
1 cup	250ml
1 ¼ cups	300ml
1 ½ cups	375ml
1 ⅔ cups	400ml
1 ¾ cups	450ml
2 cups	500ml
2 ½ cups	600ml
3 cups	750ml

WEIGHT

Standard	Metric
½ oz	15g
1 oz	30g
2 oz	60g
3 oz	90g
4 oz	125g
6 oz	175g
8 oz	250g
10 oz	300g
12 oz	375g
13 oz	400g
14 oz	425g
1 lb	500g
1½ lb	750g
2 lb	1 kg

OVEN TEMPERATURE

Fahrenheit	Celsius	Description
225°F	110°C	Cool
250°F	120°C	Cool
275°F	140°C	Very slow
300°F	150°C	Very slow
325°F	160°C	Slow
350°F	180°C	Moderate
375°F	190°C	Moderate
400°F	200°C	Moderately Hot
425°F	220°C	Hot
450°F	230°C	Hot

cook's notes

This book consists of all my favourite things – the things I love to eat! Some are new dishes that I have made up and some are from my childhood, some take me right back to my gran's kitchen when we were kids and others just make me really happy.

I discovered a quote by George Bernard Shaw recently which I loved. 'There is no love more sincere than that of food,' said the man himself, and this is what *Love Food* is all about.

The cooking times in this book are a suggestion, no two ovens are the same and you will know your own oven.

Always use fresh ingredients, my only exceptions are tinned beans and tomatoes, use good quality ones, they are perfect and they make life a lot easier. You can never have enough butter and cream, use lots of olive oil and good homemade chicken stock. Take the time to make your own stock, it really is worth the time and effort. It's one of the most nurturing flavours you can add to any dish, not to mention being very good for you.

Lashings of homemade mayonnaise are out of this world and the recipe in this book (see page 53) is very yummy! Homemade salad dressings are the key to creating the tastiest salads. And indulge yourself in the easy selection of scrumptious puddings…

I hope you enjoy cooking and eating these dishes as much as I have!

Tina Bester

TO MY FAMILY AND FRIENDS

♥

thanks

My mom, dad (RIP) and my gran have had a huge influence on the food I love and cook, so a gigantic thank you to all three of you. Thank you to all my friends and family for enjoying my food with such enthusiasm. To Craig and Libby and the Quivertree team for once again being so lovely to work with and producing another gorgeous book.
To Vicki, your words are pure genius. To Robyn, for your meticulous editing once again.
To Mdu, Asanda, Siti, Nono, Connie and Odi, you are all invaluable to me.
Thank you!

RECIPES & STYLING TINA BESTER **WORDS** VICKI SLEET **PHOTOGRAPHS** CRAIG FRASER
DESIGN & PRODUCTION LIBBY DOYLE **DTP** SUZANNE GULDEMOND
COPY EDITOR ROBYN ALEXANDER **SCANNING** RAY'S PHOTO CONTROL

QUEEN OF TARTS LOGO DESIGN FRED SWART, STUDIO STAMP 082-341-2819
PROPS SUE LANGEMAN 072-186-1403

FIRST PUBLISHED IN 2010 BY QUIVERTREE PUBLICATIONS
PO Box 51051 · Waterfront · 8002 · Cape Town · South Africa
T: +27 (0) 21 461 6808 · F: +27 (0) 21 461 6842 · E: info@quivertree.co.za
www.quivertreepublications.com · www.quivertreeimages.com

THIS EDITION PUBLISHED IN 2012 BY PAVILION
AN IMPRINT OF ANOVA BOOKS GROUP LTD
10, SOUTHCOMBE STREET, LONDON W14 0RA
www.anovabooks.com